Introduction to the Theory of Yin-Yang

Yin-Yang

2nd edition

陰陽

By

Kevin Dewayne Hughes

Ace Kiwami Publications
Introduction to the Theory of Yin-Yang

1st edition Copy Right 2014
2nd edition Copy Right 2020

Hughes, Kevin Dewayne, 1974 –
Information for Energy Arts; Martial Arts; Qi Gong; Yoga; Taiji; Reiki; Massage; Chinese Medicine; Chinese Philosophy; Chinese Culture; Acupuncture; Acupressure.

Dedication

To my mother J. Diane Mudge whose loving support and dedication has enabled me to study these martial arts and energy arts that I enjoy so much.

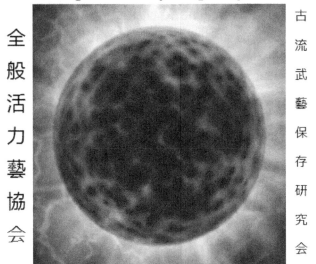

Zempan Katsuryokugei Kyokai

全般活力藝協会

古流武藝保存研究会

Universal Energy Arts Society

The original Universal Energy Arts Logo.

The Universal Energy Arts Society (Zempan Katsuryokugei Kyokai) is an organization founded by Kevin Dewayne Hughes and is dedicated to harmonizing the different energy arts. It began as a division of the Old School Martial Arts Preservation and Research Society (Koryu Bugei Hozon Kenkyukai) as a separate section to preserve the use of Martial Qi Gong, Nei Gong, and Yoga in the martial arts. It is still dedicated to these goals but is now also dedicated to helping non-martial artists learn these energy arts for the cultivation of health and vitality.

Old School Martial Arts

保存研究会

古流武藝

Research and Preservation Society

Original Logo for the Koryu Bugei Hozon Kenkyu Kai

The Koryu Bugei Hozon Kenkyukai (Old Schools Martial Arts Preservation and Research Society) has as its mission to research and preserve old school methods of the martial arts. This is not the preservation of individual schools but the preservation of technique. As sport based martial arts grow in popularity, the true martial arts are in decline. It is the goal of this organization to make sure that the old combative methods survive into the future with the help of like-minded individuals and groups.

Kevin Dewayne Hughes from 1st edition of text

Kevin Dewayne Hughes is Kaicho (organization head) and Kaiso (founder) of the Koryu Bugei Hozon Kenkyukai as well as its divisions. He is an expert in the martial and energy arts of the orient. His knowledge is sought after around the world and he has been recognized as one of the leading experts in Japanese and Okinawan martial arts by not only his peers but by the old grand masters of the previous generation. His knowledge is most often sought by those wishing to change their martial arts system from the modern competition sports based techniques of today to the tried and tested battlefield and self-protection techniques of the past. He is also recognized as one of the leading weapons experts and many schools seek his advice and knowledge on how to incorporate a weapons program into their curriculum. Martial arts schools also seek him out to learn more about the energy arts upon which the advanced martial arts are based and to incorporate energy arts training into their martial arts programs.

As of the publication of this text, Kevin Dewayne Hughes has formed the Tenkidokan or Hall of the Way of Heavenly Energy to teach Martial Art, Energy Arts, and related activities such as fitness and self-defense. The Tenkidokan is now the top of the structure and the Old School Martial Arts Research and Preservation Society and the Universal Energy Arts Society fall under the Tenkidokan.

To find and follow us:

www.tenkidokan.com

Introduction

The theory of Yin-Yang and the Five Elements theory are at the core of ancient Chinese philosophy and thought. These two theories are thus essential to truly understand the martial arts and energy arts of China. Even those martial arts and energy arts of cultures derived from Chinese cultural such as those of Okinawa, Japan, and Korea also have roots in these two theories. Therefore, any martial artist or energy artist should learn and understand these two theories.

Please note that Yin-Yang theory is more properly called Tai Chi theory as the so-called Yin-Yang symbol is actually called the Tai Chi symbol. It is from the Tai Chi symbol and theory that the martial art of Tai Chi Chuan Fa derives its name.

The theory of Yin-Yang is based on the idea that everything in the universe is constantly undergoing changes due to the interaction of Yin and Yang. This interaction causes the universe to create and destroy. Without the interaction of Yin and Yang, the universe would not exist.

In essence, Yin-Yang Theory (Tai Chi Theory) is a model of how the universe works that is very similar to the Big Bang Theory. I have hypothesized over the years that Georges Henri Joseph Édouard Lemaître, the Belgian Catholic priest, mathematician, astronomer, and professor of physics at the Catholic University of Louvain, who proposed the Big Bang Theory had also studied Tai Chi Theory (Yin-Yang Theory). Unfortunately, he died before I was born and thus asking him this was impossible.

Back to the Tai Chi. Yin-Yang can be compared to forces in the understanding of modern science. Things with mass are then the building blocks or materials used to create things and are ultimately the things that are destroyed. The Five Elements theory supplies the materials for creation and destruction by the interaction of Yin and Yang.

Wuxing = five elements

Yin Character

The Chinese character for Yin

This is the character for Yin. It is the negative principle of Yin-Yang. In Mandarin it is Yin but in Cantonese it is Jam. In Japanese it is In and Korean it is Eum. Yin represent passiveness, feminine, inside, darkness, and other such things.

Yang Character

The Chinese Character for Yang

This is the character for Yang. It is the positive principle of Yin-Yang. In Mandarin it is Yang but in Cantonese it is Joeng. In Japanese it is Yo and in Korean it is Yang. Yang represents activeness, masculine, outside, light, and other such things.

History
No one is sure when the theory of Yin and Yang was first introduced to the Chinese culture. It more than likely predates recorded history. There is evidence from clay pots dated at over 10,000 years old that have markings that may represent Yin-Yang.

The concept of Yin and Yang was sophisticated by the time of the Zhou Dynasty (1122-249 B.C.). During the Zhou Dynasty the Zhouyi (more commonly called the I-Ching) or Book of Changes was written. It is one of the oldest and foremost classical Chinese texts. It uses Yin-Yang theory via eight trigrams to explain the universe and everything in it.

The eight triagrams (Bagua).

The eight triagrams, also called the Bagua, are a combination of solid and dashed lines. The dashed lines are Yin and the solid lines are Yang. Combinations of these triagrams along with five elements theory eventual leads to the ten thousand things, which is essentially everything in the Universe.

In the time since the Zhouyi, the theory has continued to evolve and many symbols have been used to show the workings of Yin and Yang in the universe. Its concepts can be used to explain everything from geology to the workings of the human body. The concepts can be applied to health and medicine. Nutritional guides have been made using these concepts and even the cycle of life can be expressed with Yin and Yang.

Some Interesting Notes
Please note that Tai Ji and Tai Chi are the exact same thing. Tai Ji is the Pinyan romanization and Tai Chi is the Wade-Gyles romanization of the Chinese Characters used to write Tai Chi. It is important to know both the Pinyan and Wade-Gyles romanization methods. Pinyan is the preferred romanization method of modern China. However, a lot of old texts as well as translations of classics have been done with Wade-Gyles romanization.

The Chinese characters for Tai Chi

If you are a person who does Shotokan Karate of another Japanese Karate derived

14

from Shotokan, you will notice that these are the same kanji (Chinese characters used in Japanese writing) used to write the basic kata called Taikyoku. If you are a student of the Korean Karate system of Tae Kwon Do, then you will notice that these are the same Hanja (Chinese characters used in Korean writing) used to write the names of poomse called Taeguk.

The Tai Ji
Yin and Yang are usually depicted by a symbol called the Tai Ji and is the origin for the name of the martial art Tai Ji or Tai Chi. The most common symbol is seen below this paragraph. In this symbol the large circle encompassing the symbol represents the whole universe. The tear drop shaped fields represent Yin and Yang. Yin is represented by black and Yang is represented by white. The specific purpose of the tear drop shape is to represent the increasing and decreasing of Yin and Yang in the universe. They are swirled about indicating the transformation between Yin and Yang. Within each tear drop there is a field of the opposite color. The white dot in the black Yin field indicates that within Yin there is Yang and the black

dot in the white Yang field indicates that within Yang there is Yin.

The Tai Ji (Tai Chi) Symbol. Commonly called the Yin-Yang Symbol.

An older Tai Ji symbol is seen below this paragraph. In this symbol everything is pretty much the same except a central circle is added. This central circle represents what is called the Wuji. The Wuji is the concept of emptiness or the primordial nothingness from which the universe was spawned. In Taoist thought, the Wuji gives rise to Tai Ji and gives oneness. This oneness then gives rise to all things.

The Tai Ji with the Wuji concept included.

For example chapter 42 of the Tao Teh Ching states:

> Tao produces one.
> One produces two.
> Two produces three.
> Three produces a myriad of things.
> Myriad of things, backed by yin and embracing yang.
> Achieve harmony by integrating

their energy.
What the people dislike.
Are alone, bereft, and unworthy.
But the rulers call themselves
with these terms.

Here we have the Tao producing one. The
Wuji is the one in the Taiji with the Wuji.
From the Wuji are spawned Yin and Yang.
Yin and Yang are a duality or two. From
these three, Wuji, Yin, and Yang come all
things in the universe which is still
represented by the encompassing circle.

Other symbols have been used to depict the
Tai Ji but add nothing to the definition of Yin
and Yang. The symbol below is similar to the
common Tai Ji Symbol above of but
emphasizes the swirling of Yin and Yang.

Another rendition of the Tai Ji Symbol

Four Types of Changes
Yin and Yang are constantly changing and this gives rise to the shape and function of the universe. Yin-Yang theory can be summarized into four basic themes: 1. Yin Yang Opposition (Yin Yang Duili), 2. Yin Yang Interdependence (Yin Yang Hugen), 3. Yin Yang Waxing and Waning (Yin Yang Xiaozhang), and 4. Yin Yang Transformation (Yin Yang Zhuanhua).

Yin-Yang Opposition
According to ancient Chinese philosophy everything in the universe is interrelated and everything has an inseparable but opposing counterpart. This is seen in most everything today in modern physics. The atom is composed of positive protons and negative electrons. Yes, the neutron has no counterpart on the surface but inside it too is made of smaller particles of opposing charges. Magnets have a north and a south pole. All interactions and phenomena seem to have some dualistic property.

Even in Biology there is a dualistic nature of higher organisms to be female (yin) or male (yang). In Hinduism, there is a version of Yin-Yang theory called Yoni and Linga. Yoni is represented by female genitalia and Linga is represented by the male genitalia. Yoni is therefore similar to Yin and Linga is similar to Yang.

Now, do not thing the Yin and Yang is exactly the same as Yoni and Linga. They are indeed similar, but there are differences as well. One purpose of the Universal Energy Arts Society is to explore these difference and similarities and generate a unified theory.

Table of Opposites in Yin-Yang Theory

Yin	Yang
Negative	Positive
Passive	Aggressive
Dark	Light
Moon	Sun
Resting	Active
Earth	Heaven
Matter	Energy
Flat	Round
Right	Left
North	South
West	East
Feminine	Masculine

Although Yin represents weakness while Yang represents strength, do not think of it as meaning that everything associated with Yin is weak and everything associated with Yang is strong. There are things that are Yang that are weak and there are things that are Yin that are strong. Also realize that there is always Yin within Yang and Yang within Yin.

Yin-Yang Interdependence

Yin and Yang must coexist. The one cannot exist without the other. Take any container for example. The inside of the container is considered Yin and the outside is Yang. If either the Yin or the Yang part of the container did not exist, then the container does not exist. Yin and Yang cannot exist without the other and must depend on the other for existence.

The Cannon of Medicine, a Chinese book of medicine says:
Yin in the interior is the guardian of yang, yang in the exterior is the activator of yin.

Take note of the above saying when considering the difference between internal and external martial arts. Are they really different?

The flow of electricity would not work without yin and yang theory. In electrical flow there is a positive electrode and a negative electrode. Now physicists messed this one up. They thought protons were the primary things driving electricity and they called protons positive and electrons negative. So in conventional current flow, the electricity travels from the positive pole to the negative pole. In this case the positive pole would be positive for one and be the excited and active pole. This would make the positive electrode the yang electrode. The negative electrode is the passive and not excited according to conventional electron flow. Thus the negative electrode is the Yin electrode.

However, it is the electron that flows in electrical circuits. We will ignore hole flow found in semiconductor devices for now. The negative electrode is where all the electrons are stored. They are excited and ready to move to the positive electrode. Therefore, the negative electrode is Yang and the positive electrode is Yin. The flow of electricity would not happen if Yin and Yang were not interdependent.

Also, take note, that although Yin and Yang seek a balance, a true balance is undesirable. A balanced Yin and Yang in an electrical circuit means the electricity stops flowing. A dead battery is the result of the Yin and the Yang coming to a balance. The same goes for life. When the Yin and the Yang comes to a total balance in a life, the life ceases; death results.

When energy arts and martial arts seek to balance the Yin and the Yang, they seek a dynamic balance where Yin and Yang are transforming back and forth between each other through the point of equilibrium.

The Opposition and the Interdependence of Yin and Yang: Martial Arts Perspective
From a martial arts perspective, do not think that the passive Yin is less powerful than the Aggressive Yang. The two are equal in power and use and complement each other. Yang relies of brute force to win but Yin relies on yielding to win. Aikido is such an art that

uses yielding to win and it can be more effective than using brute force.

Wushu = Bujutsu = Martial Arts

Also from a martial arts perspective, the concept of punching and chambering the other fist shows how Yin and Yang work together. The punching hand is considered aggressive and it is thus Yang. The hand going to chamber is passive and thus Yin. From a basic view point only the Yang hand is doing the actual attacking but the Yin hand is helping to generate scission which increases the power of the blow. Yin and Yang have just worked together in harmony. However, from an advanced martial arts perspective, the Yin hand is actually holding part of the target and pulling the target in. In this case, Yin and Yang are working together, but with this application the Yin hand is just as aggressive as the Yang hand and just as responsible for the damage to the target as the Yang hand. In fact, the use of the Yin hand as a pulling hand causes a positive synergy.

Yin-Yang Waxing and Waning
The state of Yin and Yang in the universe is not static. Yin and Yang constantly change

with each other. As Yin increases, Yang decreases and vice versa. It is this constant flow between Yin and Yang that powers the universe. The motion of the Sun across the heavens demonstrates this concept. As the Sun rises the sky becomes brighter and Yang increases but the darkness of the night disappears and Yin decreases. Then as evening approaches the Sun sets and daylight fades which is decreasing Yang. The darkness of the night comes in and Yin increases. Note that this also relates to why the Moon is Yin and the Sun is Yang.

The goal of energy arts and martial arts training is to increase the maximal amount of Yin and Yang energy. This seems to be impossible with the fact that one decreases and the other increases. The mindset needs to be different. Take the Tai Ji Symbol and make is larger so that when Yin increases there is a larger increase and when Yang increases there is a larger increase.

Yin-Yang Transformation
Under extreme conditions, Yin and Yang can change from one to the other. The example in the Yin-Yang Waxing and Waning section

does not show Yin becoming Yang and vice versa. The light, which is Yang does not become darkness, which is Yin.

A simple example would be traveling due north. The northward direction is Yin. But if one were to travel north to the North Pole and then keep going, suddenly one is heading south. Yin suddenly became Yang. The North Pole is an extreme condition on this path of travel. It is the point where there is no going north or south. Once passing the extreme, the direction of travel is suddenly Yang.

Another simple example to help clarify the extreme condition can be seen in throwing a ball straight at a wall. The velocity of the ball toward the wall is Yang velocity. It is Yang because active action has to be put into it to move the ball. Once the ball hits the wall there is an instantaneous moment that the ball goes to zero velocity and then accelerates in the other direction. At this point, due to the direction change, the ball goes to infinite acceleration and receives a Yin velocity in the opposite direction. It is Yin because no active action was taken to accelerate the ball in the opposite direction.

One more example is due to gravity. Gravity is a passive force. No action is needed to cause gravity to work. Throwing a ball in the air takes an active action to work. As the ball receives its initial velocity form the person accelerating it, the ball immediately begins to decelerate. The Yang velocity starts to decrease due to the Yin acceleration due to the force of gravity. At some point in the air, the Yin acceleration cancels out the Yang velocity and this is when the Yin-Yang transformation occurs. Yin velocity now takes over and increases due to the acceleration due to gravity. When the ball hits the ground, it will be like the wall example above. Depending on the material of the ball and the material of the ground, the ball can go through several oscillations of Yin-Yang transformation.

Balancing Yin and Yang

According to the theory of Yin-Yang the two opposing forces are interdependent on each other. This means that everything a person does must occur in pairs. If a person inhales then exhalation must occur. Activity must be paired with rest. Ultimately this leads to balance.

The theory also states that as one increases the other decreases and vice versa. If a person spends too much time working one area, then another area will suffer. This applies not only to activities but also to what is consumed. Again this leads to balance.

For example: Weight lifting increase Yang while stretching increases Yin of the muscles. Too much Yang and the joints will be stiff and injury prone. Too much Yin and the joints will be too loose and injury prone.

Just note that in the energy arts, that the Chinese say long muscles means long life. This is because the Yang of the body tissues increases with age so the aging process is fought by increasing the Yin of the body tissues. This is one of the concepts in Yin Yoga and in the style of Yoga that I developed called Aayuh Yoga or Life Yoga with an emphasis on longevity.

In everything we do we should strive to achieve balance be it physical, mental, or spiritual. Go for the dynamic balance for maximal benefits.

Dietary Balance of Yin and Yang

Foods can be categorized as Yin foods and Yang foods. If a person consumes too many Yang foods, then the body will become too Yang or vice versa. If the body becomes too Yang or too Yin then health problems set in. For example, spicy foods are considered Yang. Eating too many Yang foods without enough Yin foods to provide balance tends to lead to indigestion and in extreme cases can lead to gallbladder problems up to and including the need to remove the gallbladder. If a person is eating Mexican food, salsa is a Yang food and should be balance with avocado, which is a Yin food. The table below lists some foods and designates if they are Yin or Yang as well as which organ the food supports.

Another way to write wushu

List of food by organ and if it is Yin or Yang

Organ	Yin	Yang
Heart	Whole grain rice; Mushrooms; Chamomile; Jujube seed	Red meats
Spleen	**Rice congee; Cooked oats**	**High Carb vegetables**
Lungs	Dairy; Sweet rice; Pear; Apple	Onions; Peppers
Kidneys	**Shellfish; Kidney beans; Bone marrow; Seaweed**	**Kidney offal; Royal jelly**
Liver	Tofu; Berries; Seaweed; Rhubarb root	Ginger Horseradish

Emotional Balance of Yin and Yang

The emotions should be balanced as well. Anger, a Yang emotion, can lead to stress related health problems. But joy, a Yin emotion, can also bring about problems in life such as becoming oblivious to reality.

There are more than two emotions and a person can experience multiple emotions at one time. The concept of centering is used to discuss balancing the emotions and the Five Elements theory needs to come into the discussion to better understand the emotions in energy arts.

Centering means to bring your emotions and thoughts to a neutral state. Slow deep breathing is used at the beginning of any of the energy art classes such as Yoga, Qi Gong, and Tai Ji. During this time of slow deep breathing, one should clear the mind of distracting thoughts so that the mind can focus on the energy work at hand. Also, one should bring all emotions back to neutral or center. Allow anger, joy, sadness, and all emotions to come to a neutral state. If something causes one to be angry, allow the thoughts of the anger to clear the mind and allow the feeling of anger to leave the body. By so doing, center is achieved and the energy will flow better for the energy work at hand.

Emotions cause a disturbance in the mind. This induced chaos makes it more difficult to lead the energy. By centering the emotions, the mind becomes calm and tranquil. From here, the mind is ready to direct the energy flow in the body.

In traditional Chinese thought, there are five emotions and each one relates to one of the five elements. The five emotions are: sadness, fear, anger, happiness, and worry. Each element relates as follows: fire = happiness; earth = worry; metal = sadness; water = fear; wood = anger. As this is a topic for another book, I will just state that the five emotions are in balance when the five Yin organs are in balance; more on this topic in a future book.

Physical Balancing of Yin and Yang
When training the body, it is easy to over train one side and under train the other side. The over trained side occurs because it gets favored due to better energy flow into the activity being done. This can be seen in writing.

Most people are right-handed. But are we actually born to be right-handed while only a few are born to be left-handed. It is my belief that we become right-handed due to favoring the right hand for a lot of activities. This desire to favor comes from better energy flow in the more used side. Weather we are born with higher flow on the right side than the left is yet another question, but I believe that everyone has the potential to be ambidextrous.

I have even experimented with this. I have taken my martial arts classes and my energy arts classes and taught things on the left side of the body for weeks then asked them to duplicate on the right side. It gave the expected result. All the right-handed students were left-handed on the task I trained them on and had difficulty doing it on their right side.

One of the experiments I did with the martial arts students involved the use of the sai. I taught them a kata I created for this experiment. There was a special trick with the sai not seen in any kata that I teach from the weapons systems I have learned. This trick was only done on the left side and never on the right. The students were unaware that I was teaching them a special kata for the sole purpose of an experiment on my energy flow hypothesis about left or right hand dominance. After a months training, I asked them to do the trick with the right hand and they simply could not duplicate it and they wanted to go back to doing it with the left hand.

This experiment is one reason, why I require my students to learn the normal and mirror image of all the forms (kata) that they do.

In each experiment that I did, be it with martial arts student or energy arts students, the results were the same.

In another experiment I did it with people who were not my students but kids at a camp I was a camp councilor at. I took a class of ten people who were all right-handed. I taught them a fine motor task on the left hand and had them do it on the left hand for many repetitions every day for a week. After the week, I taught them to do the technique on their right hand for another week; their dominate side. When the students were free to do as they wished they went back and favored the left hand.

Vitality

In order for one to become ambidextrous, one must train both sides of the body equally. From the first attempt at a new activity train each side exactly the same number of times. Unfortunately, some activities can be so complex that learning one side takes many repetitions and to avoid confusion only one side is initially learned. This leads to an imbalance of the energy flow to both sides. In order to correct this situation, the less efficient or weaker side should be trained two to three times as much as the dominate side until both sided are equal. Once equality is achieved then both sides should be trained the same number of times.

Yin and Yang within Yin and Yang
Training the body or the mind can appear to be balanced on a macroscopic scale, but if one were to look at the training at a

microscopic scale one will see imbalances in the training. For example when doing a Martial Arts, Qi Gong, Tai Ji, or Yoga sequence, one should do the sequence with the normal and mirror images. That means that if the sequence starts of the right side then, the same sequence should be done opposite by starting on the left side. This would balance Yin and Yang at the macroscopic level.

However balance is not fully achieved. In order to balance the microscopic level one must start the sequence with the normal image then do the mirror image one day and then the next day start with the mirror image and then do the normal image. The microscopic can also be balanced by switching which image to start with at weeklong intervals. That is one week start with the normal image then the next week start with the mirror image. Another method would be to do the normal image one day and the mirror image the next day.

Now the common Tai Ji symbol shows that there is Yin within Yang and Yang within Yin and at the surface would only indicate that there are only two levels. Unfortunately there are even more levels. For example the sequences have a super macroscopic level with which to balance Yin and Yang. In any of the arts, there are multiple sequences to learn. Always starting with the same sequence and running through them in the same order will create an imbalance. (For those who do a martial art like Karate, this means do not start with kata 1 then kata 2 then kata 3 and so on. Rather start at kata 1 on day one and run all the kata. Then on day 2 start with kata 2 and run all the kata and end with kata 1. Proceed as such until the last kata is the first one you do). One reason is that the body will be fresh on the first sequence and fatigued by the last sequence. In order to avoid this imbalance in training one should change up which sequence is done first. Now you can also change the order but that can become quite cumbersome. I suggest that the sequences be placed in a circular pattern and simply change the starting position on the circle after a complete rotation.

Now three levels of balancing Yin and Yang have been presented for training. That is the macroscopic level, the level, and microscopic level. However, a fourth level of Yin and Yang can be introduced. It is not uncommon for people to study more than one art. For example it is very common for people to study Qi Gong and Yoga or to study Qi Gong and Taiji or even study all three. In the same way as the super macroscopic level, one needs to alternate which art they train first during the day.

Yin and Yang divisions of the Body

The body is divided into sections based on the theory of Yin-Yang as well as divided based on the Five Elements theory. The first table below lists the body divisions by Yin and Yang pairing. The organs can also be categorized as Yin and Yang as shown in the second table below.

Yin and Yang body divisions

Yin	Yang
Interior	Exterior
Front	Back
Body	Head
Below waist	Above waist
Structure	Function
Body fluids	Energy
Organs	Skin and muscles
Anterior	Posterior
Conservation	Transformation

Yin and Yang organ pair

Yin	Yang
Heart	Small intestine
Lung	Large intestine
Liver	Gall Bladder
Spleen	Stomach
Kidney	Bladder
Pericardium	Triple Warmer

A Word for Martial Artists

Pay attention to Yin and Yang as it relates to the human body. When in combat one should attack Yin and Yang. Attack a Yin energy meridian and a Yang energy meridian. For example: strike the front side and also the backside.

Concluding Remarks

It is my hope that you find this information informing and that you will seek out the aid of a qualified instructor to assist you in training in either the martial arts or energy arts or both. I can be contacted at the following web address.

www.tenkidokan.com

Please feel free to contact me with regards to the information within this publication and I will do my best to answer each one.

I would also like each reader to note that the theory of Yin-Yang is ultimately a model of how the universe works. Although the theory is a philosophy and adopted by major schools of philosophy such as Taoism and Confucianism, which have evolved from being schools of philosophy into religions, does not make this theory a religious idea. It is a separate idea, used by religion. It is as much a theory as the Theory of Plate Tectonics is in modern day geologic and scientific understanding.

It is an old scientific theory based upon human understanding of the material world long ago. Although modern scientific theories surpass Yin-Yang theory in reliability and understanding, it is still important for the martial artist and energy artist to know. This theory is needed to develop an understanding of the Chinese classics and the classics of Chinese subcultures so that the martial arts and energy arts described in these classics can be fully appreciated and the concepts described can be properly applied.

Thank You for Reading and Enjoy Your Training,

Kevin Dewayne Hughes
2nd Edition 20 July 2020

Printed in Great Britain
by Amazon